unity in diversity

VIRTUES OF MY HEART

Written and Illustrated by Melissa López Charepoo

Text and Illustrations
© 2021 Melissa López Charepoo

First published 2021. Reprint 2026.

ISBN 978-1-971750-25-5 (paperback)

To all who make the world a better place by striving for

unity in diversity.

Have you ever wondered what **unity in diversity** means?

Unity in diversity means to come together as one human family, even though we are all different and unique in our own ways. We are not afraid of our differences; instead, we see them as a strength. Unity is a good quality, or virtue of our hearts. Practicing unity helps us develop many other virtues as well. As we free our hearts from any kind of prejudice or ideas that are not based on reason, we can honor, respect, and love every human being.

We can strive to be unified with everyone who crosses our path!

I have a diverse family. We all have different opinions, ideas, and likes. To strive for unity, I free my heart from the prejudice that only my opinion matters. When I speak, I always keep in mind the feelings of others and I share my thoughts with **tact**.

How do you strive for unity by sharing your ideas and opinions with **tact**?

I belong to a diverse extended family. My family is made up of people of different races, ethnic groups, and cultural backgrounds. To strive for unity, I free my heart from the thinking that my skin color, race, or ethnic group is superior to others. Instead, we enjoy learning about and celebrating all the races and backgrounds that are a part of our family. I **honor** the **beauty** that our diverse family creates, as I believe that really there is only one race: humanity.

How do you strive for unity by **honoring** the **beauty**
in the diversity of humanity?

We live in a diverse building. In my building, there are people with physical and mental challenges. To strive for unity, I free my heart from thinking that only people that have the same physical and mental abilities as I do can have a normal life. Instead, I show **compassion** and **caring** as we strive to create a living place that is comfortable and safe for everyone.

How do you strive for unity by **caring** and showing **compassion** for people with different physical and mental abilities?

I attend a diverse school. In my school I have peers of different ages, genders, and orientations. To strive for unity, I free my heart from any feeling of prejudice that only boys like me can get good grades or do best at sports. I believe everyone has been created equal, and so I treat my peers with **fairness** and **friendliness**.

How do you strive for unity by treating everyone with **fairness** and **friendliness**?

I have a diverse group of friends. Each of us has different talents. Talents are special and unique gifts given to each one of us. To strive for unity, I free my heart from feeling that my talents are more important and valuable than others. Instead, I support my friends in the things they like to do as we hope one day to use our talents for **service** to humanity.

How do you strive for unity by developing your talents and helping others to do the same to **serve** humanity?

I live in a diverse community. People that have different belief systems live here. To strive for unity, I free my heart from the prejudice that only through my religion can a person lead a good life. Instead, I **respect** all beliefs and embrace all religions as one, from one Creator.

How do you strive for unity by **respecting** all beliefs?

I live in a diverse country. People with different social and economic levels live here. Some people have more money than others and can afford more material things. I free my heart from the prejudice that people only matter according to the material things they have. Instead, I treat everyone with **dignity**. I recognize the nobility in each person.

How do you strive for unity by treating everyone with **dignity**?

We live in a diverse world. In every country of the world, you will find people of different races, cultures, genders, orientations, social and economic levels, and with different beliefs, opinions, likes, ideas, and talents. Beyond freeing my heart from any prejudices that I may have; I also strive for a fair society where everyone has the same rights and opportunities. Therefore, I stand for **justice**. After all, without a fair and just society we cannot achieve unity in the world.

How do you strive for unity by standing for **justice**?

As you can see, we have diversity in every aspect of our lives, but we can strive for **unity** with everyone that crosses our path. By striving for unity in diversity, our heart develops many virtues, such as tact, honor, beauty, caring, compassion, fairness, friendliness, service, respect, dignity, and justice.

Our hearts are always joyful when we strive for **unity in diversity**!

Glossary

Beauty – a sense of reverence and wonder for a combination of qualities such as color, shape, and form

Caring – showing kindness and concern for others

Compassion – caring for others

Dignity – being worthy of honor and respect

Fairness – just treatment of others without discrimination

Friendliness – having a bond of mutual affection with someone

Honor – to regard with great respect and esteem

Justice - being fair in everything we do

Kindness - the quality of being friendly, generous, and considerate

Prejudice - an opinion of an individual, group, or race that is not based in truth

Respect – a deep admiration for someone or something

Service – the act of helping others without expecting anything in return

Tact – being sensitive to the feelings of others

Unity – being part of a whole; togetherness

Virtue – behavior showing high moral standards; good qualities of our hearts

References:

The Virtues Project Cards

Oxford English Dictionary

Heartfelt thanks to:

My beloved husband Darioush Charepoo for all his support.

Our dearly loved boys for being the inspiration.

Leanna Guillén Mora for helping with proofreading and editing the book.